THE MYSTERY OF THE CROOKED IMP

TALES OF FAYT

THE
DEMON'S WATCH
NEEDS

YOU!

Written by
Conrad

Illustrated by
David Wyatt

It is a tale of their strangest enemy yet.

A tale of the Crooked Imp . . .

THE MYSTERY OF THE CROOKED IMP

TALES OF FAYT

Written by

Conrad Mason

Illustrated by

David Wyatt

PORT FAYT

THE BRIG
A BEACHED PRISON SHIP WHERE FAYT'S ROUGHEST CRIMINALS END UP. THE ONES THAT GET CAUGHT, ANYWAY.

LIGHTHOUSE

DOCKSIDE
AH, THE SALT SPRAY! THE FRESH AIR! THE STENCH OF ROTTEN FISH! DOCKSIDE IS THE BUSTLING HEART OF PORT FAYT. OLD WORLD TRADERS MIX WITH SHELLFISH HAWKERS, REVENUE MEN AND EVEN THE ODD PIRATE.

MARLINSPIKE QUARTER
HOME TO FAYT'S LEGENDARY FAIRY MARKET AND THE GROTTIEST TAVERNS IN TOWN. DO YOURSELF A FAVOUR - DON'T TAKE A STROLL HERE AFTER DARK.

THE PICKLED DRAGON
TRY THEIR GUTSPILLER GROG FOR A NIGHT YOU'LL NEVER REMEMBER.

THE RUSTY ANCHOR
THE SAFEST LODGING HOUSE IN TOWN, SO LONG AS YOU SLEEP WITH ONE EYE OPEN.

CROSSTREE QUARTER
PORT FAYT'S BEST SHIPWRIGHTS LIVE HERE, BUILDING WAVECUTTERS AND GALLEONS TO CROSS THE EBONY OCEAN. COULD BE HANDY IF YOU NEED TO LEAVE IN A HURRY.

THE MANTICORE PLAYHOUSE
WORD IS A DANGEROUS GANG HAVE TAKEN OVER THIS ABANDONED THEATRE. AVOID!

MER WAY

FLAGSTAFF QUARTER
ONLY THE FILTHY RICH LIVE HERE - THE GOVERNER, MERCHANTS FROM THE TRADING COMPANIES AND THE BETTER CLASS OF CRIMINAL.

BOOTLES' PIE SHOP
HEADQUARTERS OF THE DEMON'S WATCH

THE BRANDYSNAP VELVETHOUSE
A HOT CUP OF VELVETBEAN HERE CAN SOLVE ANY PROBLEM.

THALIN SQUARE

AND THERE IT IS...
PORT FAYT! BEST STUDY THIS MAP CAREFULLY. IF YOU SET FOOT IN THE WRONG PART OF TOWN, YOU'LL FIND YOURSELF IN THE BRIG, OR WORSE. JUST STICK WITH OL' CROCKLEWICK AND YOU WON'T GO FAR WRONG.

NOW, PREPARE YOURSELF FOR A TALE WITH MORE TWISTS THAN A KRAKEN'S TENTACLE... THE MYSTERY OF THE CROOKED IMP!

MIDNIGHT IN PORT FAYT.
HOME TO HUMANS, TROLLS, ELVES...

AND *FAIRIES*.

FISHSTICKS!
LATE AGAIN!

SQUAWK!

GAH!

SWWWIIISSSHHHHHH

THALIN'S
BREECHES!
THAT WAS
CLOSE.

THIRD DRAGON
ALONG, *THIRD* DRAGON
ALONG...*GOTCHA!*

EVENIN'
FELLA!

THWACK!

THE *RATTIGAN* HOUSEHOLD. FLAGSTAFF QUARTER, PORT FAYT.

SOME HOUSE! YOU COULD FIT A *DRAGON* IN HERE!

TABS. LEAVE THE TALKING TO ME, *REMEMBER*?

BUT—

YOU'LL BE A WATCHMAN *ONE* DAY. FOR NOW, WATCH AND *LEARN*.

THERE YOU ARE! THANK *THALIN!*

CAPTAIN *NEWTON*, AT YOUR SERVICE.

CELIA RATTIGAN. *SNUFF?*

EURGH! NO THANK YOU!

TABS...

HMM... SIT DOWN –sniff– YOU ARE HERE BECAUSE LAST NIGHT, OUR DARLING BABY *CLARENCE* WAS STOLEN FROM US –atchoo!

OUR DRIVER WAS TAKING HIM TO HIS AUNT'S HOUSE, BUT –

WILL YOU LEAVE THAT ALONE?

SORRY.

...BUT THIS MORNING WE HEARD THAT THE CARRIAGE NEVER ARRIVED.

ANY IDEA WHAT HAPPENED?

MAYBE THE DRIVER TOOK THE BABY. OR *ANOTHER* SERVANT.

HAVE YOU GOT ANY? BESIDES THE MAID?

TABITHA!

HMPH. JUST TRYING TO HELP.

ALL WE WANT IS CLARENCE RETURNED TO US. THE REWARD WILL BE *SUBSTANTIAL.*

THE *MONEY* DOESN'T MATTER, MA'AM. WE'LL FIND YOUR CHILD.

AH, THE *VELVETBEAN* ARRIVES. *AT LAST.* POUR IT OUT, JOANNA.

SUGAR?

I... I'M SORRY, WE'VE...ER... *RUN OUT.*

NONSENSE! THERE WERE TWO FULL BAGS ONLY YESTERDAY. *HONESTLY, GIRL!*

JOANNA, WHERE IS MY BLASTED...

OH! APOLOGIES, I DIDN'T KNOW WE HAD GUESTS.

NO NEED TO EXPLAIN, *DEAR.*

WE'LL BRING YOUR LITTLE'UN BACK SAFELY, MR RATTIGAN.

AH... YOU MUST BE A *TROLL,* THEN? SPLENDID.

CAPTAIN NEWTON, I HOPE WE CAN KEEP THIS BUSINESS BETWEEN OURSELVES. DON'T WANT A *SCANDAL* ON OUR HANDS, EH?

DARLING...

WE'LL HANDLE IT.

NOW, THIS CARRIAGE DRIVER...

HIS NAME IS *WHELK.* UNSAVOURY CHARACTER. WE SHOULD NEVER HAVE TRUSTED A *DWARF.*

DARLING!

P-PARDON ME, BUT YOU COULD TRY WHELK'S LODGING HOUSE? IT'S THE *RUSTY ANCHOR* ON BREAKNECK ALLEY, OFF *MER WAY.*

SOON AFTERWARDS...

D'YOU THINK WHELK *DID* TAKE THE BABY?

WE'LL SEE.

...OR THE AUNT...

MAYBE.

IT'S FUNNY THE *RATTIGANS* WEREN'T IN THE CARRIAGE WITH HIM.

HM.

AND THEY DIDN'T EVEN SEEM THAT *UPSET!*

I RECKON THEY'RE NOT AS *RICH* AS THEY MAKE OUT.

THAT VASE WAS *FILTHY!* ONLY *ONE* SERVANT FOR THAT BIG OL' HOUSE, AND–

RUSTY ANCHOR

TABS, I *KNOW* YOU WANT TO HELP.

BUT DON'T GET CARRIED AWAY, *UNDERSTAND?* STICK WITH ME AND YOU'LL BE FINE.

WE'RE LOOKING FOR A *DWARF,* NAME OF WHELK.

UPSTAIRS. FIRST ON THE LEFT.

IT'S NOT FAIR. I *NEVER* GET TO...

OH, THALIN...

LOOK!

13

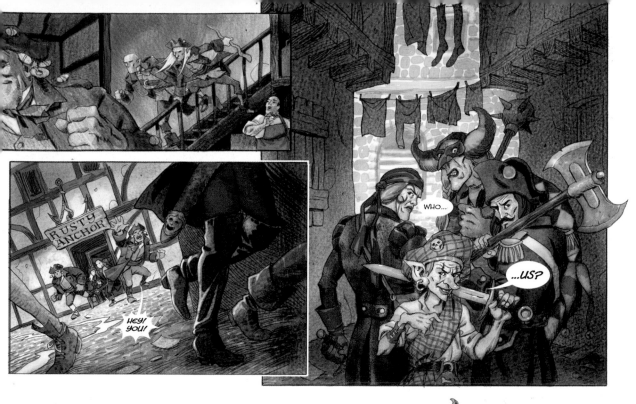

OI! YOU SNEAKY LI'L PRIVY ROACH!

BOK!

I TOLD YOU TO STAY INSIDE!

I ALWAYS HAVE TO STAY INSIDE!

IT'S NOT FAIR. FRANK AND PADDY GET TO FIGHT!

THEY'RE OLDER THAN YOU. AND THEY'RE TROLLS.

WHAT ABOUT HAL? HE'S NOT THAT MUCH OLDER THAN-

HE'S A MAGICIAN, TABS!

NEWT!

SO LET ME GUESS. THE CIRCUS IS IN TOWN?

VERY FUNNY. I KNOW WHO YOU ARE. DEMON'S WATCH, AIN'T IT? I SEEN THEM SHARK TATTOOS. YOU LOT ARE WORSE THAN THE MILITIA!

WELL, THE BOSS'LL BE COMING FOR YOU NOW.

RIPP!

WATCH YER OWN BACKS, WATCHMEN!

OOPS.

AND LOOK - HE FORGOT HIS FISH SLICE!

AN HOUR LATER. *BOOTLES' PIE SHOP*. HEADQUARTERS OF THE DEMON'S WATCH.

SO WHO *WERE* THOSE BLACK-HEARTED BLOATERS?

LOOKED LIKE CLOWNS, DIDN'T THEY? IF YOU'D ONLY HELD ONTO THAT SKINNY ONE...

LITTLE BLIGHTER WAS SLIPPERY AS AN EEL.

PASS ME A *PIE*, WILL YOU PADDY?

HE MENTIONED A BOSS... WHICH MEANS THEY WERE *ORDERED* TO KILL WHELK.

THE ONLY WITNESS TO THE KIDNAPPING.

DON'T TAKE A MAGICIAN TO FIGURE IT OUT, EH, HAL?

WHOEVER THEIR BOSS IS— *THAT'S* WHO TOOK BABY CLARENCE!

WHELK SAID SOMETHING BEFORE HE DIED. HE SAID WE SHOULD FIND *'THE CROOKED IMP'*.

HMM. THAT'S A FUNNY NAME.

YOU HEARD OF A CROOKED IMP, JON?

NO.

THEN WE'LL ASK AROUND. MAYBE THIS IMP'S THEIR BOSS. MAYBE IT WAS *HIM* WHO TOOK CLARENCE AND SENT HIS THUGS TO SILENCE WHELK.

I'M TABITHA, BY THE WAY. YOU CAN CALL ME TABS.

SPOON. PLEASED TO MEET YOU, MISS!

THANKS FOR THE CAKE ~munch~ I HAD SOME SUGAR BUT THAT STINKY OLD SEAGULL MADE ME DROP IT.

NEVER MIND. BUT SHOULDN'T YOU BE GETTING BACK TO YOUR MASTER?

I AIN'T GOT NO MASTER! I'M A FREE FAIRY, ME. NOT ONE OF THEM ERRAND BOYS WHAT GET BOSSED AROUND ALL DAY LONG!

SO HOW DO YOU GET SUGAR? I THOUGHT FAIRIES COULDN'T DO WITHOUT IT.

I GET BY. THERE'S THIS CLUMSY SERVING MAID AT THE BRANDY SNAP VELVETHOUSE. AT THE END OF THE DAY, SHE SWEEPS ALL THE SPILT SUGAR OUT INTO THE ALLEY...

AND GUESS WHO'S WAITING FOR IT?

SMART.

I WISH I HAD A FAIRY LIKE YOU. NEWT WON'T LET ME HAVE ONE, THOUGH. HE NEVER LETS ME DO ANYTHING FUN.

WELL, I, ER... BEST BE GOING, MISS. THANKS FOR THE CAKE!

WAIT, DON'T...

NO ONE'S EVER CALLED ME THAT BEFORE!

...GO.

AS DUSK FALLS IN THE MARLINSPIKE QUARTER...

ADMIT IT, HAL. IF ANYONE CAN TELL US WHO THIS *CROOKED IMP* FELLA IS, IT'S *JEB THE SNITCH.*

AYE. BUT HE'S *OUR* SCALLYWAG.

I STILL DON'T LIKE IT. JEB WOULD SELL HIS OWN MA FOR AN OGRE'S TOENAIL. HE'S A *SCALLYWAG.*

JEB THE – WHO?

HE'S A *GOBLIN.* A SMALL-TIME CROOK. NASTY PIECE OF WORK, BUT HE *KNOWS* THINGS.

SO WHY DON'T THE BLACKCOATS *ARREST* HIM?

THE MILITIA? BECAUSE THEY'RE ABOUT AS MUCH USE AS A RUBBER CUTLASS. *SEE?*

THAT'S WHY THE DEMON'S WATCH WAS SET UP IN THE FIRST PLACE. *SOMEONE'S* GOT TO LOOK AFTER THIS TOWN.

THERE IT IS. THE *PICKLED DRAGON.*

IF JEB AIN'T IN HERE, I'LL EAT MY HAT. AND FRANK'S, TOO.

PICKLED [DRAGON]

AND... THEY'RE OFF!

FIVE DUCATS ON THE RED CRAB!

SHIFT YER SHELL!

MOVE IT, NIPPER!

SCUTTLE

SCRTCH

23

EVENING, JEB.

HANDS OFF, YER STINKIN'...

OH, NEWT! AIN'T SEEN YOU IN DRAGONS' YEARS!

NOT WATCHING THE RACE, JEB?

NO NEED, MATE!

'TWEEN YOU AND ME, THE BLUE CRAB'S GOING TO WIN.

THE BLUE CRAB WINS!

HOW DID HE —

DON'T ASK.

WE RAN INTO A BUNCH OF *THUGS* AT THE RUSTY ANCHOR, JEB.

THUGS IN MAKE-UP.

AND FUNNY CLOTHES, TOO. LIKE CLOWNS, OR SOMETHING.

SOUNDS LIKE THE *ACTOR'S* MEN. BUNCH O' LOONIES IF YOU ASK ME...

WHO'S THE ACTOR?

YOU AIN'T HEARD O' THE *ACTOR?!* WELL THEN, SIT TIGHT AND LISTEN UP.

COULD THE ACTOR AND HIS MEN BE *WORKING* FOR SOMEONE...

SOMEONE CALLED THE *CROOKED IMP?*

NEVER HEARD OF NO CROOKED IMP.

TELL YOU WHAT, THOUGH. THE ACTOR'S GANG MEET EVERY NIGHT AT THIS OLD *PLAYHOUSE* IN THE MARLINSPIKE QUARTER. GET THERE EARLY, WITH PLENTY O' GUNS, AND YER'LL CATCH HIM PUTTING ON HIS MAKE-UP. *CREEPY SCUMBAG.*

COURSE IF I WAS YOU, I'D FORGET IT.

IF THE ACTOR *IS* WORKING FOR SOMEONE... SOMEONE *BIG* ENOUGH AND *BAD* ENOUGH TO BOSS THAT MANIAC TROLL AROUND...

THEN WHOEVER IT IS, YOU DON'T WANT TO BE ON THE *WRONG SIDE* OF 'EM.

AND AT THAT MOMENT...

I FEAR WE HAVE A *PROBLEM.*

MY POOR *PLAYERS*... THEY KILLED THE DWARF, BUT ALAS, THEIR EXIT WAS *RUDELY* INTERRUPTED.

BY THE *BLACK-COATS?*

BY THE *DEMON'S WATCH.*

THEN DEAL WITH IT. AND *QUICKLY.*

HAVE NO FEAR. IF THE WATCHMEN PERSIST, I'LL TREAT THEM TO ONE OF MY *PERFORMANCES.*

AND MUCH AS I *HATE* TO SPOIL THE ENDING...

...I CAN ASSURE YOU THAT THEY ALL *DIE.*

...BUT JEB SAID TO TAKE GUNS!

AYE, *GUNS*, NOT *CANNONS*.

WE'RE JUST GOING FOR A *QUIET WORD* WITH THE ACTOR. LAST THING WE NEED IS A *SHOOTOUT*.

WHAT ABOUT ME? I'M NOT EVEN ALLOWED TO COME IN THE FIRST PLACE!

TABS, WE'VE DISCUSSED THIS. YOU'VE NEVER BEEN IN A FIGHT BEFORE.

WHAT ABOUT THE *RUSTY ANCHOR*?

THAT WAS A *SCUFFLE*, AND I TOLD YOU TO STAY OUT OF IT.

CLIK!

YOU'LL BE SAFER *HERE*, TABS

YOU'LL GET A BREAK FROM OUR UGLY MUGS...

...AND THINK OF ALL THE *PIES* YOU CAN EAT!

ENOUGH.

LET'S GET GOING. WE'LL CATCH THE ACTOR BEFORE HIS *GANG* TURNS UP. FIND OUT IF HE'S WORKING FOR THIS *CROOKED IMP*, AND IF THEY HAVE THE BABY.

HMPH!

27

FAIRIES... SO IT WASN'T THE ACTOR WHO TOOK CLARENCE *AFTER* ALL...

WE FOUND IT PINNED TO THE FRONT DOOR. WILL YOU GIVE IT TO CAPTAIN NEWTON? I REALLY SHOULD BE GOING...

WAIT! WHAT WILL THE RATTIGANS DO NOW?

I DON'T –

THE GOVERNOR CAN'T JUST TELL THE MERCHANTS TO GIVE UP ALL THEIR FAIRIES, CAN HE?

ER...

SO IT'S UP TO US. WE HAVE TO FIND THE BABY BEFORE –

NO!

I MEAN... IT'S NOT MY PLACE, BUT SURELY... IF YOU GO AFTER THE FAIRIES THEY MIGHT... WELL, CLARENCE IS AT THEIR MERCY.

I'M SORRY. I *HAVE* TO GO.

MAW'S TEETH!

THE SHOW'S OVER.

PHILISTINES!

WHAT THE... WHERE'S HE GONE?

YOU WERE TALKING TO SOMEONE. WAS IT THE CROOKED IMP?

I BEG YOUR PARDON?

DROP THE ACT, MATEY. WHELK TOLD US TO FIND THE CROOKED IMP. JUST BEFORE HE DIED.

WHELK TOLD YOU?

AYE. THE CROOKED IMP'S YOUR BOSS, AIN'T HE?

WHAT'S HE DONE WITH LITTLE CLARENCE?

HMM. HA HA. HA HA HA HA!

WHAT'S FUNNY?

THE PLOT THICKENS! I'M AFRAID MY PATRON IS NOT THE CROOKED IMP. BUT I DO KNOW WHERE THE IMP CAN BE FOUND.

BOSS? WHERE ARE YOU? WE'RE COMING!

HUZZAH – THE PERFORMANCE IS SAVED! YOU'LL LOVE THIS NEXT SCENE. PLENTY OF BLOOD AND GUTS. MOSTLY YOURS.

GOOD OL' TABS!

SHARPER THAN A BAG O' DRAGONS' TEETH!

BUT YOU DON'T UNDERSTAND. I DID IT TO *PROTECT* HIM!

YOU SEE, CLARENCE IS NO ORDINARY BABY...

FROM THE DAY HE WAS BORN, THINGS *HAPPENED* AROUND HIM. *STRANGE* THINGS...

TIN SOLDIERS MARCHING BY THEMSELVES. A ROCKING HORSE FLOATING IN MID AIR...

IT GOT WORSE AND WORSE, UNTIL ONE DAY A DOCTOR CAME TO SEE HIM. A DOCTOR WHO KNEW ABOUT *MAGIC.*

HE SAID THAT CLARENCE WAS SPECIAL. A *NATURAL MAGICIAN.* MOST PEOPLE HAVE TO *LEARN* MAGIC. BUT THEY CAN *NEVER* BE AS POWERFUL AS ONE WHO'S BORN WITH IT FLOWING THROUGH THEIR VEINS.

AND IT'S RARE. *EXTREMELY* RARE.

THE RATTIGANS COULDN'T BELIEVE THEIR LUCK. THEY'RE IN *TERRIBLE* DEBT, AND THEY THOUGHT CLARENCE WAS THE SOLUTION.

THEY'D NEVER WANTED HIM IN THE FIRST PLACE, AND TO THE RIGHT PERSON HE WAS WORTH THOUSANDS OF DUCATS.

SO THEY DECIDED... TO *SELL* HIM.

YOU CARE ABOUT THE BABY, DON'T YOU?

OF COURSE. I'M NOT A *MONSTER.* AND IF THE RATTIGANS HAD GOT THEIR WAY, WELL...

...WHO KNOWS *WHAT* WOULD HAVE HAPPENED TO HIM? I COULDN'T LET THEM DO IT.

I WAS GOING TO LOOK AFTER CLARENCE, IN *SECRET.*

I THOUGHT THE RANSOM NOTE WOULD STOP YOU FROM INVESTIGATING. BECAUSE IF THE RATTIGANS FOUND OUT *I* WAS INVOLVED...

47

YOU, MY DEAR, WILL SHORTLY LEARN THE ERROR OF YOUR WAYS.

AND YOU... LITTLE CLARENCE. SO MUCH TROUBLE FOR SUCH A TINY FELLOW.

BUT FEAR NOT! I KNOW SOMEONE WHO'LL BE *VERY* PLEASED TO SEE YOU.

SNATCH

WHO IS IT? WHO ARE YOU WORKING FOR?

HA HA HA! MY DEAR CAPTAIN NEWTON! YOU CAN'T POSSIBLY EXPECT ME TO TELL YOU THAT.

HOW CAN YOU BE SO CRUEL?

CLARENCE IS JUST A BABY, FOR THALIN'S SAKE. YOU WERE A CHILD ONCE! PLEASE, HAVE SOME PITY!

A POOR PERFORMANCE INDEED! THE *WORLD* IS CRUEL, MY DEAR, AND NO ONE'S EVER PITIED *ME!*

A *SPECTACLE* TO DELIGHT AND ENTERTAIN YOU!

NOW, IF YOU'LL ALL COME ALONG. I'VE A LITTLE SURPRISE IN STORE.

Spoon? You there?
Good. Keep your head down.
GOING TO MAKE US WALK THE PLANK, ARE YOU? HOW ORIGINAL.
A COMEDIAN! SPLENDID! I DID CONSIDER IT, BUT ALL THAT SPLASHING AROUND IN THE DARKNESS MAKES FOR A DREARY SHOW.
STILL, 'EATEN ALIVE BY SHARKS'. THERE IS SOMETHING DELICIOUSLY DRAMATIC ABOUT IT.
SO I DECIDED...
...TO BRING MY OWN!
CHOMP
WHAT? NO APPLAUSE? NO ENCORE?
YOU MUST BE JOKING.
PHILISTINE! DO I LOOK LIKE A JOKER TO YOU? NO, I AM AN ARTISTE!
I MUST CONFESS, I AM DISAPPOINTED. I HAD HOPED YOU WOULD APPRECIATE MY LITTLE SHOW.
PERHAPS THIS WILL HELP.

LET HER GO, YOU MANIAC!

AND *RUIN* MY *GRAND FINALE?* ABSOLUTELY *NOT!*

Look up, quick! Is that...

Urgh! It's that stinky seagull!

LISTEN, WHEN I SAY GO, YOU SCREAM AND FLY STRAIGHT AT THAT TROLL. GOT IT?

WHAT DO YOU —

GO!

WWWWAAAAAAAAAAAAAAHHHH.!

THE NEXT MORNING.

NOK, NOK

JOANNA? *JOANNA?*

JOANNA! I HAD TO OPEN THE DOOR *MYSELF,* GIRL! WHERE IN THALIN'S NAME HAVE YOU *BEEN?*

MAYBE *WE* CAN EXPLAIN.

THAT GIRL... THREE HOURS LATE! *OUTRAGEOUS.*

AND IT'S ABOUT TO GET WORSE...

MAKE US SOME VELVETBEAN, JOANNA. AT ONCE!

AH, SO YOU THOUGHT YOU'D SHOW UP, DID YOU GIRL? HOW *LUCKY* WE ARE! HOW EXTREMELY –

MR RATTIGAN. MRS RATTIGAN. WE KNOW.

YOU – YOU DO?

KNOW WHAT?

THAT YOU TRIED TO SELL YOUR BABY TO ONE OF THE WORST CROOKS IN PORT FAYT.

THAT CLARENCE WAS KIDNAPPED ON THE NIGHT HE WAS TO BE HANDED OVER.

AND THAT YOU CALLED US IN TO INVESTIGATE...

...HOPING WE'D JUST RETURN THE BABY AND KEEP QUIET.

WELL. THAT'S NOT HAPPENING.

I- HOW *DARE* YOU! YOU'VE GOT NO RIGHT TO... I MEAN, *REALLY...*

WHAT DO YOU INTEND TO DO?

JOANNA IS NO LONGER YOUR SERVANT. WE'LL FIND HER WORK ELSEWHERE, AND IN THE MEANTIME SHE'LL LOOK AFTER THE CHILD.

SHE CARES ABOUT CLARENCE, MORE THAN YOU *EVER* HAVE.

BEST SAY GOODBYE. YOU'LL NOT SEE HER AGAIN.

BUT.... YOU'RE NOT ARRESTING US?

THE BLACKCOATS ARE WAITING OUTSIDE. THEY'LL ESCORT YOU TO THE DOCKS, WHERE YOU'LL BOARD A SHIP, SET SAIL AND *NEVER* RETURN TO PORT FAYT.

COUNT YOURSELVES LUCKY. BUT IF YOU EVER TRY TO HURT JOANNA...

IF YOU EVER *TOUCH* HER...

I'LL BE PAYING YOU A VISIT...

...AND I DON'T EXPECT YOU'LL LIKE IT VERY MUCH.

SLAP!

NOW, PROMISE YOU'LL TAKE GOOD CARE OF HIM, WON'T YOU JOANNA?

I PROMISE.

HEY, MISS!

GOT ANY SUGAR?

SPOON!

THAT WAS A MEAN TRICK YOU PLAYED WITH THE SEAGULL. BUT I'M ALL RIGHT.

MA SAYS IT WAS DEAD CLEVER OF ME TO KNOCK OUT THAT TROLL! SHE SAYS I'M A HERO!

WELL. I MEAN, IT WAS MY IDEA.

THPBT! OH, ALL RIGHT. WE CAN BOTH BE HEROES.

TIME TO GO, TABS.

THANKS FOR LETTING ME AND MY FAMILY OFF THE HOOK, MISTER. YOU'RE A GENT.

WILL I SEE YOU AGAIN?

RECKON SO, MISS. MAYBE NEXT TIME YOU'LL BE A PROPER WATCHMAN AND ALL!

MAYBE.

TILL NEXT TIME, THEN.

AYE. TILL NEXT TIME.

THE *BRIG*. LATER THAT DAY.

THE HOODED MAN. HE WASN'T THE CROOKED IMP.

SO WHO WAS HE?

HMPH. HA HA.

HA HA HAAA!

COME ON, TALK. YOU'VE NOTHING TO LOSE.

IS HE A HUMAN?

AMATEURS! HE'S NO HUMAN.

AN ELF THEN?

HA HA HAAA! HE IS SOMETHING ELSE, CAPTAIN NEWTON.

SOMETHING ELSE ENTIRELY.

WHAT DO YOU MEAN?

THERE ARE STORIES WHISPERED IN THE SHADOWS... BUT IN TRUTH, NO ONE KNOWS *WHAT* HE IS, NOR WHENCE HE CAME. NO ONE WISHES TO KNOW.

THE BOOTLE BROTHERS!

AGE
28
SPECIES
TROLLS
WEAPON
CUTLASSES
SPECIAL SKILL
INCREDIBLE STRENGTH
FAVOURITE PIE
WHATEVER'S GOING

A PAIR OF TROLL TWINS, FRANK AND PADDY LOVE GOOD JOKES, GOOD FRIENDS AND GOOD HOT PIES WITH PLENTY OF GRAVY!

AGE
38
SPECIES
HUMAN-OGRE
WEAPON
BLACK QUARTERSTAFF
NICKNAMED 'THE BANSHEE'
SPECIAL SKILL
LEADERSHIP
FAVOURITE PIE
CRAB

CAPTAIN NEWTON

THE CAPTAIN OF THE WATCH HAS OGRE BLOOD FLOWING IN HIS VEINS. HE FIGHTS WITH A QUARTERSTAFF, BUT GIVES NO QUARTER.

OLD JON

THIS ANCIENT ELF DOESN'T TALK MUCH, BUT DON'T BE FOOLED. HE'S AS SHARP AS A DRAGON'S TOOTH.

AGE
SOME SAY AS OLD AS THE SEA
SPECIES
ELF
WEAPON
A PLAIN WOODEN CUDGEL
SPECIAL SKILL
WISDOM
FAVOURITE PIE
FLOUNDER

THE ADVENTURE CONTINUES!

THE DEMON'S WATCH

CONRAD MASON

A Tale of the Demon's Watch

THE GOBLIN'S GIFT

Conrad Mason

FOLLOW THE FURTHER EXPLOITS OF
TABITHA AND THE DEMON'S WATCH IN CONRAD
MASON'S TALES OF FAYT NOVELS...

TALES OF FAYT

THE
HERO'S TOMB

Conrad Mason

The Mystery of the Crooked Imp: Tales of Fayt
is a
DAVID FICKLING BOOK

First published in Great Britain in 2015 by
David Fickling Books,
31 Beaumont Street,
Oxford, OX1 2NP

978-1-910200-42-1

1 3 5 7 9 10 8 6 4 2

David Fickling Books supports the Forest Stewardship Council (FSC),
the leading international forest certification organisation. All our titles
that are printed on Greenpeace-approved FSC-certified paper carry the FSC logo.

MIX
Paper from
responsible sources
FSC® C020872
www.fsc.org

DAVID FICKLING BOOKS Reg. No. 8340307

A CIP catalogue record for this book is
available from the British Library.

Printed and bound in Great Britain by Polestar Stones.